Gwenda Turner

TEACHING
BEARS
TO COUNT

For my Mother, John, Judith, Leigh & Isabel.
Many thanks to Erin, Elle, Jade, Larissa,
Jessie and Barbara's Bears.

THIS BOOK BELONGS TO

....

Gwenda Turner

TEACHING
BEARS
TO COUNT

PUFFIN BOOKS

1 one	**2** two	**3** three	**4** four	**5** five
6 six	**7** seven	**8** eight	**9** nine	**10** ten

1
one

one dog

1
one

2
two

3
three

4
four

5
five

6
six

7
seven

8
eight

9
nine

10
ten

2
two

two eggs

1	**2**	**3**	**4**	**5**
one	two	**three**	four	five
6	**7**	**8**	**9**	**10**
six	seven	eight	nine	ten

3

three

three kittens

1 one 2 two 3 three **4 four** 5 five
6 six 7 seven 8 eight 9 nine 10 ten

4 four

four balloons

1 one 2 two 3 three 4 four 5 five

6 six 7 seven 8 eight 9 nine 10 ten

5
five

five chocolate fish

1 one
2 two
3 three
4 four
5 five
6 six
7 seven
8 eight
9 nine
10 ten

6

six

six pikelets

1	2	3	4	5
one	two	three	four	five
6	**7**	8	9	10
six	**seven**	eight	nine	ten

7
seven

seven presents

1 one
2 two
3 three
4 four
5 five
6 six
7 seven
8 eight
9 nine
10 ten

8
eight

eight pegs

1 2 3 4 5

one two three four five

6 7 8 9 10

six seven eight **9 nine** ten

9
nine

nine candles

1 2 3 4 5

one   two   three   four   five

6 7 8 9 10

six   seven   eight   nine   ten

10

ten

ten hats

1 one

2 two

3 three

4 four

5 five

6 six

7 seven

8 eight

9 nine

10 ten